POSITIVE STEPS

Understanding Feelings

by Susan Martineau

with illustrations by Hel James

A+

Smart Apple Media

Published by Smart Apple Media
P.O. Box 3263, Mankato, Minnesota 56002

Printed in the United States of America at Corporate Graphics in North Mankato, Minnesota.

Library of Congress Cataloging-in-Publication Data
Martineau, Susan.
 Understanding feelings / by Susan Martineau with illustrations by Hel James.
    p. cm. -- (Positive steps)
Includes index.
 ISBN 978-1-59920-494-9 (library binding)
 1. Emotions in children--Juvenile literature. 2. Expression in children--Juvenile literature.
I. Title.
 BF723.E6M37 2012
 155.4'124--dc22

                                                                            2011011725

Created by Appleseed Editions, Ltd.
Designed and illustrated by Hel James
Edited by Mary-Jane Wilkins
Picture research by Su Alexander

Picture credits
Contents page Monkey Business Images/Shutterstock; 4l Leah-Anne Thompson/Shutterstock, r thewfinalmiracle/Shutterstock; 5 Gladskikh Tatiana/Shutterstock; 6 Morgan Lane Photography/ Shutterstock; 7t grublee/Shutterstock, b Orange Line Media/Shutterstock; 8 background Daniel Boom/ Shutterstock; 9 background Benis Arapovic/Shutterstock; 10 Hay Wiremedia/Shutterstock, 10-11 background Alhovic/Shutterstock, 11t Roman White/Shutterstock, c Dmitry Naumov/Shutterstock, b Shell114/Shutterstock; 12 Rob Marmion/Shutterstock; 13 AraBus/Shutterstock; 15l Jupiter Images/ Thinkstock, tr Danila/Shutterstock, b Kakzs/Shutterstock, Georgy Markov/Shutterstock; 16 Morgan Lane Photography/Shutterstock, 16-17 background P Kruger/Shutterstock, 17t Mandy Godbehear/ Shutterstock, c Anatoliy Samara/Shutterstock, b Rossario/Shutterstock; 18t Sparkling Moments Photography/Shutterstock, b Tomasz Trojanowski/Shutterstock; 19t YoYo_Sic/Shutterstock, b Bernad/ Shutterstock; 20 YanLev/Shutterstock; 21t Lara65/Shutterstock, b Jacek Chabraszewski/Shutterstock; 22 Noam Armonn/Shutterstock, 22-23 background Fotosav/Shutterstock, 23 Zurijeta/Shutterstock; 24tl Tomasz Markowski/Shutterstock, tr Raisa Kanareva/Shutterstock, bl R Gino Santa Maria, br Stuart Miles/ Shutterstock; 25t Sonya Etchison/Shutterstock, bl David Davis/Shutterstock, br Monkey Business Images/ Shutterstock; 27 MaszaS/Shutterstock; 28-29 background Lakov Kalinin/Shutterstock; 32 Noam Armonn/Shutterstock
Front cover: Leah-Anne Thompson/Shutterstock

DAD0048
3-2011

9 8 7 6 5 4 3 2 1

Contents

I feel great!

Why Do I Feel Like This?

A feeling is something we feel inside us, such as anger, happiness, or sadness. We all have many different feelings, or **emotions**, every day.

My brother drives me crazy!

I miss my dad. I'm feeling sad.

I feel really shy.

I'm so worried about . . .

I'm so jealous of her.

Holidays make me feel happy.

All these feelings are **normal**, but we need to try and **understand** them. Understanding why we feel the way we do helps us when we have feelings that worry us or are **confusing**.

LET'S TALK ABOUT . . .

Can you think of times when you have felt like these children? Can you think of some more emotions or feelings?

I'm Really Worried

Everyone feels worried from time to time. Being worried is when we think something bad is going to happen. Different people worry about different things. Something we find easy might worry someone else.

Keeping worries to yourself can make the worry worse. Worries can become so big that they make you unhappy and stop you from doing things. Sometimes being worried even makes your tummy hurt or keeps you awake at night.

I'm really worried about going on the school trip.

What if I can't sit with my friends on the bus?

What can you do?

- Try to figure out why you are worried. Maybe there is a simple answer to your worry.

- Talk to a friend, a parent, or your teacher about your worry. They will be able to help you.

- Sometimes we have to do difficult things. Try to say, "I'm **nervous** and worried, but I am determined to do this!" You will feel great when you have done it!

Tell a friend about your worries.

Don't worry, my wrist will be better soon.

Dealing with Worries

Take turns thinking of some things you worry about. Now talk about ways of dealing with them. For example, if you are worried about not being with your friends on a school trip, you could talk to your teacher about it.

I Hate You!

When we feel really angry with someone or something, we may say or do things we do not really mean. Sometimes we might hit someone or throw and break things because we are so mad.

I'm gonna kill you!

I hate you!

Being angry is normal, but we have to keep our anger under **control**. We must not let our anger take over the way we behave.

Anger can be a good thing if it makes us stick up for what is right. If we feel angry when we see someone being bullied, then we are more likely to help them.

Stop it! You're being a bully.

LET'S TALK ABOUT . . .

Write down or draw some of the things that make you angry. Are they really worth getting so angry about? Think about how you feel if someone is angry with you. It can be scary!

If someone doesn't want to play my game

My little brother is always taking my stuff.

When my mom scolds me

What can you do?
- Instead of losing your temper, try to keep calm. Walk away or take some deep breaths.

- Talk to people instead of shouting at them. Think before you speak.

- When other people get angry, don't shout back. Try to help them calm down.

I Feel Jealous

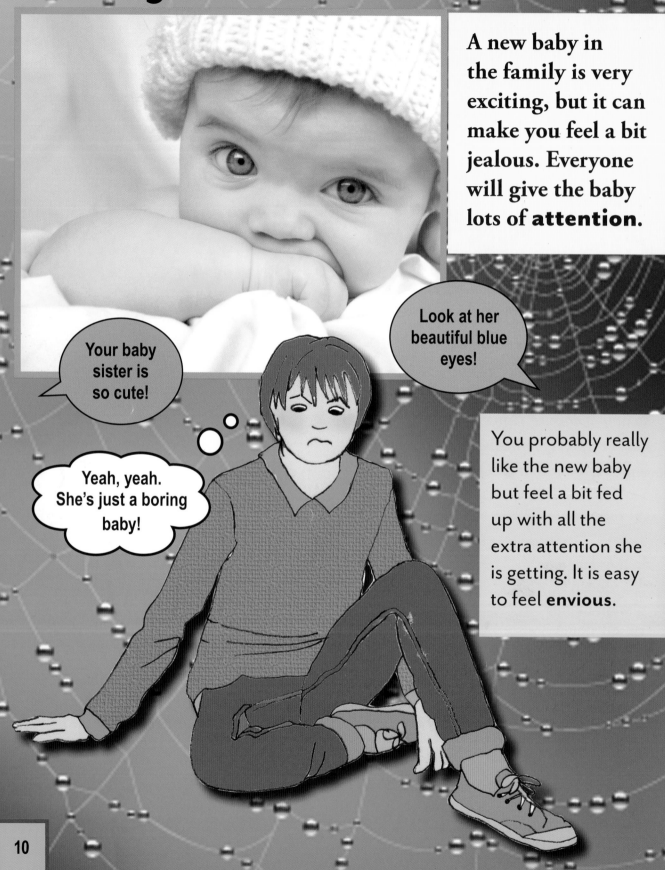

A new baby in the family is very exciting, but it can make you feel a bit jealous. Everyone will give the baby lots of **attention**.

Your baby sister is so cute!

Look at her beautiful blue eyes!

Yeah, yeah. She's just a boring baby!

You probably really like the new baby but feel a bit fed up with all the extra attention she is getting. It is easy to feel **envious**.

What can you do?

Feeling jealous of a new baby is quite natural, but remember the baby isn't there to replace you. Your parents still love you just as much.

Don't let jealous feelings make you unhappy with what you have. Remember all the good things you have. Someone else may be feeling jealous of you for having a cute baby brother or sister!

He has this really cool new bike.

LET'S TALK ABOUT . . .

Can you think of times when you have felt jealous of other people? It can be hard when someone else always seems to have things that you would like.

I wish I had shoes like hers.

Feeling Shy

Lizzie is feeling unsure of herself at her new school. She feels **shy** about talking to the other children and making new friends. She's writing to her cousin about it.

Hi Lucy,

I like my new school but I don't have any new friends yet. I usually play on my own at recess. I'm a bit scared of talking to the others and don't know what to say to them.

I'm looking forward to seeing you at Gran's during the summer.

Love from Lizzie

Which words below describe how Lizzie is feeling? Have you felt like this? Do you know anyone who might feel like this?

outgoing

scared

confident

quiet

shy

lonely

What can you do?

- Try to be **outgoing**. Smile and say hello to other people. You will start to feel less shy.

- Maybe think of some questions you could ask people about hobbies or favorite movies.

- If you know that someone is feeling shy about joining in a game, be kind and invite them to take part.

Hi, Lizzie. Do you want to play?

Hello, I'm Lizzie.

I'm So Sad

When pets die, we feel very sad. We miss them and wish they were still alive. We find it very hard to believe they are gone.

You might feel so sad that you cannot imagine ever feeling happy again. It will take time, but you will have happy feelings again.

Saying goodbye to someone makes us feel sad. Try to look forward to the next time you will see them and remember the good times you have had.

LET'S TALK ABOUT . . .

It is normal to feel very unhappy when a pet dies. Sometimes other things happen to make us feel sad too. Can you think of some? Whenever we feel sad, it can help to try and remember happier times.

What can you do?

- Talk to your friends and family when you are feeling sad.

- If your friends are sad, try to understand why. Think of ways to cheer them up.

- If a pet has died, you could make an album of pictures of the pet.

Feeling Happy, Feeling Glad

Having fun with friends and family makes us feel happy. We certainly feel happy when it is our birthday and everyone is giving us presents!

LET'S TALK ABOUT . . .

Birthdays are not the only times we feel glad. Can you think of some other things that make you happy? Does making other people feel happy make you happy too?

What can you do?

When we feel happy, it is good to share this and to help others feel cheerful too. If you see someone looking unhappy, invite them to join in a game or talk to them. See if you can make them smile!

Try to remember happy times when you are feeling worried or sad.

vacations

playing soccer with friends

watching a favorite movie

The last day of school!

It Was So Embarrassing!

Sometimes we do things that make us feel embarrassed. Other people sometimes say or do things that embarrass us. When we are embarrassed we feel as though everyone is looking at us and laughing at us.

Feeling embarrassed can make us want to disappear.

Oh no, I just called the teacher "Mom!"

I'm not wearing that. It'll make me look stupid.

I hate my new haircut.

These children all feel embarrassed. Can you think of times when you have felt the same? Ask your friends about the most embarrassing things that have happened to them and you will see that embarrassing moments happen to everyone.

I fell over in the playground.

The teacher scolded me.

What can you do?

● If you look as if you are not bothered by an embarrassing moment, other people may not even notice what happened.

● Sometimes the best thing to do is make a joke out of an embarrassing moment.

● Be kind to someone else who is feeling embarrassed. Let them know it does not matter.

Missing Someone

Charlie is writing to his big sister who does not live at home anymore. He really misses his dad since his parents split up.

Dear Claire,

I wish you were here. It's OK with Mom, but I miss Dad so much. When can we go and see him again? It was so great last time we saw him. I wish he lived a bit closer.

Hope you are all right.

See you soon,

Charlie

LET'S TALK ABOUT . . .

It is very hard for everyone when a family splits up. If you can't see your mom or dad very often, you can miss them a lot. Talking about how you feel is important. You might find this has happened to some of your friends, and they understand how you are feeling.

What can you do?

- Remember that your mom or dad still loves you and will be missing you too.

- Keep in touch as much as you can by text, e-mail, or phone.

- You could keep a diary of what you have been doing. Put in some pictures of yourself. Then you can show your mom or dad or send it to them.

I Can't Stand That

We do not always have the same feelings about things as our friends do. Sometimes we can't stand something our friends really like.

If we all felt the same about things, it would be a bit boring. Our different feelings make us the interesting people we are.

I love spaghetti!

I can't stand it.

I love looking at the stars.

I'm scared of the dark.

*What are your favorite things? What makes you feel happy, **lonely**, scared, or angry? Being honest about what we like is important, and so is working out why we like or dislike certain things. This is all part of getting to know ourselves.*

Parties are great!

I'm a bit shy at parties.

All About You

Make a booklet about yourself. Choose three things you like and three things you don't like. You could choose more if you like. Draw or write about them in your booklet. You could try to write about why you like or dislike them too.

Feel Proud of Yourself

We are all good at different things. You might be a fast reader. Perhaps your friend is great at drawing. We can all feel proud of the different things we are good at.

She's fantastic on the trampoline.

She's great on the piano.

He draws awesome cartoons.

He's amazing on a skateboard.

LET'S TALK ABOUT . . .

*Can you think of something difficult that you have had to do? You can feel proud of yourself for doing it. Perhaps you now feel more **confident** and as if you could do anything!*

Feeling proud of ourselves is a great feeling. Showing our family and friends that we are proud of them is important too.

Be a Feelings Detective!

We might know how we are feeling, but how can we tell how others are feeling? Understanding other people's feelings helps us all to get along better.

When we are trying to tell how someone is feeling we are like detectives looking for clues. The first clue is the other person's face. Are they smiling or looking sad? The way someone is sitting or standing can also tell us how they are feeling.

> We're so happy!

> **LET'S TALK ABOUT . . .**

> *Look at the children and what they are saying. Can you see how their faces and bodies tell us how they are feeling too?*

angry

sad

happy

worried

fed up

shy

How Am I Feeling?

You only need one other person to play this game, but it is fun to play with a group too. Write some feelings on pieces of paper. Turn them over. Each person takes a turn picking one. Then the player acts out the feeling on the paper using both face and body—without speaking. Everyone else guesses how they are feeling.

How Are You Feeling?

Every day we all feel lots of different emotions and feelings. Some feelings last longer than others. If we are feeling happy, we never want it to end. When we are sad, we want to feel happy again.

All of our feelings are normal. Trying to understand why we feel the way we do helps us to understand ourselves. It also helps us to understand other people.

I'm proud of myself for helping Mom with the baby.

I'm so happy because we have a new puppy!

I'm really jealous. I want one too.

What can you do?

Take a look through the book and all the feelings that are described in it. You can also look at the Glossary on page 30. Write or draw some of the things that might make you feel like that.

You could keep a Feelings Diary for a week. Describe how you feel and why on each day. You will probably find that you feel many different emotions each day.

All the bold words are explained on pages 30–31.

I was really sad when my granny was sick.

My Feelings Diary

Monday Happy
My friend came over to play.

Tuesday Shy
I had to ask a question in class.

Glossary

attention
taking lots of notice of someone or something

confident
feeling strong and brave about something

confusing
hard to understand or figure out

control
stopping something, like anger, from taking over;
being in control means being in charge.

emotion
a feeling

envious
feeling jealous of someone or something

lonely
feeling alone and without any friends

nervous
very worried or scared about doing something

normal
usual and ordinary; nothing to be worried about

outgoing
finding it easy to talk to people and make friends

hy
ot wanting to talk to people you don't know

nderstand
o know about something and what it means

Web Sites

BC Education, Health: Feelings
ttp://www.bbc.co.uk/scotland/education/health/feelings/

's My Life Games – PBS Kids: Go, Go, Diego!
ttp://pbskids.org/itsmylife/games/diego_flash.html

My Pet Died - How Can I Feel Better?
ttp://kidshealth.org/kid/feeling/thought/pet_death.html#cat20071

Index

Cheer up or I'll get mad!